Contents

Any words appearing in the text in bold, **like this**, are explained in the glossary.

What is a car?

A car is a machine that moves along on wheels. Many people use cars to go to school or work every day. Inside a car there are seats for the driver and the passengers.

Cars

Chris Oxlade

H www.heinemann.co.uk
Visit our website to find out more information about Heinemann Library books.

To order:
☎ Phone 44 (0) 1865 888066
📄 Send a fax to 44 (0) 1865 314091
💻 Visit the Heinemann Bookshop at www.heinemann.co.uk to browse our catalogue and order online.

First published in Great Britain by Heinemann Library, Halley Court, Jordan Hill, Oxford OX2 8EJ a division of Reed Educational and Professional Publishing Ltd.
Heinemann is a registered trademark of Reed Educational & Professional Publishing Ltd.

OXFORD MELBOURNE AUCKLAND
JOHANNESBURG BLANTYRE GABORONE
IBADAN PORTSMOUTH (NH) USA CHICAGO

Designed by Paul Davies and Associates
Originated by Ambassador Litho Ltd
Printed in Hong Kong/China

ISBN 0 431 10839 0 (hardback)
05 04 03 02 01
10 9 8 7 6 5 4 3 2

ISBN 0 431 10844 7 (paperback)
05 04 03 02 01
10 9 8 7 6 5 4 3 2 1

British Library Cataloguing in Publication Data

Oxlade, Chris
   Cars. – (Transport around the world)
   1.Automobiles – Juvenile literature
   2.Transportation,
   Automotive – Juvenile literature
   I.Title
   629.2'22

Acknowledgements
The Publishers would like to thank the following for permission to reproduce photographs: Allsport: Mark Thompson p20, David Taylor pp 21, 28, Mike Hewitt p29; Corbis: Bettmann p8, p12, Dave G Houser pp13, 14, W Perry Conway p15, AFP p27; Image Bank: L D Gordon p19; Quadrant Picture Library: p4, Flight p9, Felix p10, Simon Matthews p18, Pete Trafford p22; The Stock Market: p5, p11, p17; Tony Stone Images: Christopher Bissell p7, Paul Souders p21, Simon Bruty p24, David Madison p25; Trip: p16, D Palais p23, H Rogers pp6, 26

Cover photograph reproduced with permission of VW

Every effort has been made to contact copyright holders of any material reproduced in this book. Any omissions will be rectified in subsequent printings if notice is given to the Publisher.

The driver **steers** the car to the left or right using a steering wheel. The driver makes the car go faster or slower by pressing pedals on the floor with his feet.

How cars work

Most cars have four wheels. Each wheel has a **rubber** tyre. The tyres roll along the road and stop the car sliding sideways as it goes round a corner.

Every car has an **engine** which makes the wheels turn round. The engine needs **fuel** to make it work. The fuel is stored in a large **tank**.

Old cars

This car was built in 1885 by Karl Benz.
It was one of the first cars ever made.
It was like a **carriage** but it had an **engine**
instead of a horse to pull it along.

At first, very few people could afford a car. The Model-T Ford was a small car that was cheap enough for most people to buy. More than 15 million Model-T Fords were made.

Classic cars

Some cars are special because of the way they look. They are called classic cars. This Ford Thunderbird was built in the United States in 1956.

Some people collect classic cars. They spend hours polishing all the parts of the car and often display them at classic car shows.

Where are cars used?

Most cars travel along roads. Roads are hard and smooth. Lines drawn on the road show drivers where to stop to let other cars pass.

In some places there are no proper roads so cars travel on dirt tracks. The tracks are often rough and bumpy. In the winter they can become very muddy.

Four-wheel drive

In a four-wheel drive car the **engine** is joined to all four wheels. This makes it easier to drive the car along muddy or icy roads, and up very steep hills.

This car has big tyres with a chunky **rubber** pattern, called tread. The tread stops the wheels slipping in mud. The wheels also keep the bottom of the car high off the bumpy ground.

People carriers

A people carrier is a large car with six or seven seats inside. They are very useful for families with several children, and for taxi drivers.

Some of the seats in a people carrier fold down to make space for shopping or holiday luggage. A whole family and their luggage can easily fit inside.

Limousines

This long, smart car is called a limousine. The person who drives it is called a chauffeur. People hire limousines for special occasions.

The seats inside a limousine are big and comfy, like armchairs. Some limousines have a television, a telephone and a fridge for drinks.

Stock cars

In Britain, stock cars are family cars used for racing around oval **tarmac** tracks. They are allowed to bump and bash into each other. Strong bars protect the driver in case the car rolls over.

In the United States, stock cars go very fast. They are not allowed to bump into other cars. The drivers get in the car through a window instead of using the door.

Dragsters

Dragsters are racing cars that race along a short, straight track. They have huge **engines** and monster tyres covered with sticky **rubber**.

parachutes

A drag race only lasts for a few seconds, but the cars can reach 320 kilometres per hour. At the end the cars slow down using parachutes.

Racing cars

This car races against other cars on a special racing track. The cars travel at up to 350 kilometres per hour. Driving a racing car takes a lot of skill.

As the car speeds along, air goes over and under its wing. The air presses the car down, stopping it sliding about on the corners. This car is making a **pit-stop** for new tyres.

wing

Electric cars

This car looks like a normal car, but it has an **electric motor** instead of an **engine**. **Batteries** inside the car make the electricity that the motor needs.

After a few hours of driving the batteries in the electric car begin to run out of electricity. Then the car must be taken to a special **recharging** station.

Jet power

This amazing car is called *Thrust SSC*. It can travel at more than 1250 kilometres per hour. This is as fast as a fighter aircraft can fly.

Thrust SSC has **engines** taken from a jet aircraft. A jet of hot gases shoots out of the back of the engines and pushes the car forwards.

Timeline

1885   The first proper car is built in Germany by Karl Benz. It has three wheels and is driven along by a petrol **engine**. Top speed is 13 kilometres per hour.

1894   The first proper motor race starts in Paris, France. The cars race each other to Rouen.

1906   The first luxury Rolls-Royce car is sold. It is built by British engineers Charles Rolls and Henry Royce.

1908   In the USA, the Ford Motor Company builds the first Model-T Ford. The company is started by Henry Ford.

1936   The first Volkswagen Beetle is built in Germany. So far more than 20 million Beetles have been made.

1996   General Motors builds the first modern electric car that people can buy. It is called the *EV-1*.

Glossary

battery a store of electricity. The electricity is gradually used up as the battery is used.

carriage a wheeled vehicle usually pulled by a horse

electric motor a machine that powers movement using electricity. Electric cars have an electric motor.

engine a machine that powers movement using fuel. A car's engine moves the car along.

fuel anything that burns to make heat. In a car the fuel is a liquid called petrol or diesel oil.

pit-stop when a racing car stops during a race to get new tyres and more fuel

recharging putting electricity back into a battery so that it can be used again

rubber a soft substance used to make tyres for vehicles

steer to guide the direction of the car

tank a container in a car where fuel is stored

tarmac a mixture of small stones and sticky tar which makes up the smooth surface of a road

Index